What does God's voice sound like?
Psalm 29 talks about God having a voice as loud as thunder. Can you make a sound like thunder? I Kings 19:12 tells of God's voice being small and quiet. What is the tiniest whisper you can make? When and where do you hear God's voice?

T0124906

I think I hear God's voice when _____

Have you ever heard an echo? Go outside, to a canyon or an alley, or try an empty room indoors. Make some sounds, and listen for an echo. Imagine it is God calling you. What might God be saying to you?

My class went on a hike the other day.
We climbed to the top of a mountain,
and I shouted H - E - L - L - O!
I heard a voice call back
    H - E - L - L - O!
It sounded just like my voice —
only far away.

My teacher said the sound I heard
was an echo.
It was fun to hear our own voices —
We kept calling out, and the sound
from space kept calling back.

I wonder what God's voice sounds like.
    Is it deep and gruff?
    Is it soft and gentle?
    Is it loud or quiet?
I think God keeps calling out and maybe
we are the sound that calls back.
    Maybe people are God's echo.

How are you God's echo?

What does God call us to do?

Sometimes an echo doesn't have to be a sound. When we copy what another person is doing, we are "echoing" their actions.

Play an echo or mirror game with a friend: Stand facing each other. One person starts to make a movement, and the other imitates it, just as if they were a reflection in a mirror.

We read in **1 Samuel 3** about God calling a young boy named Samuel to be God's helper. God calls us to be helpers, too.

What happens when you call someone, and they don't hear you, or they don't answer? How do you feel?

How do you think God feels, when we don't listen to God, or when we don't respond?

 If you have a kite, you might fly it and feel the power of the wind.

 Make a pinwheel: Mark the center of a 6" square of paper. Cut a line from each corner to about 1/4" from the center. Bend the corners to the center, and poke a straight pin through them; poke the pin through a small button, and then stick it into the eraser of a pencil. Blow on the pinwheel or move it in the air, and watch the wind make it spin.

When the wind blows warm, making grass, trees and flowers dance, it makes my hair brush against my face.

I think the wind is God's breath moving through the world, making it come alive.

What does God's voice sound like?
Psalm 29 talks about God having a voice as loud as thunder. Can you make a sound like thunder? I Kings 19:12 tells of God's voice being small and quiet. What is the tiniest whisper you can make? When and where do you hear God's voice?

think I hear God's voice when _____

Have you ever heard an echo? Go outside, to a canyon or an alley, or try an empty room indoors. Make some sounds, and listen for an echo. Imagine it is God calling you. What might God be saying to you?

My class went on a hike the other day.
We climbed to the top of a mountain,
and I shouted H - E - L - L - O!
I heard a voice call back
   H - E - L - L - O!
It sounded just like my voice —
only far away.

My teacher said the sound I heard
was an echo.
It was fun to hear our own voices —
We kept calling out, and the sound
from space kept calling back.

I wonder what God's voice sounds like.
   Is it deep and gruff?
   Is it soft and gentle?
   Is it loud or quiet?
I think God keeps calling out and maybe
we are the sound that calls back.
   Maybe people are God's echo.

How are you God's echo?

What does God call us to do?

Sometimes an echo doesn't have to be a sound. When we copy what another person is doing, we are "echoing" their actions.

Play an echo or mirror game with a friend: Stand facing each other. One person starts to make a movement, and the other imitates it, just as if they were a reflection in a mirror.

We read in **1 Samuel 3** about God calling a young boy named Samuel to be God's helper. God calls us to be helpers, too.

What happens when you call someone, and they don't hear you, or they don't answer? How do you feel?

How do you think God feels, when we don't listen to God, or when we don't respond?

 If you have a kite, you might fly it and feel the power of the wind.

 Make a pinwheel: Mark the center of a 6" square of paper. Cut a line from each corner to about 1/4" from the center. Bend the corners to the center, and poke a straight pin through them; poke the pin through a small button, and then stick it into the eraser of a pencil. Blow on the pinwheel or move it in the air, and watch the wind make it spin.

When the wind blows warm, making grass, trees and flowers dance, it makes my hair brush against my face.

I think the wind is God's breath moving through the world, making it come alive.

2

What does God's voice sound like?
Psalm 29 talks about God having a voice as loud as thunder. Can you make a sound like thunder? I Kings 19:12 tells of God's voice being small and quiet. What is the tiniest whisper you can make? When and where do you hear God's voice?

I think I hear God's voice when _____

Have you ever heard an echo? Go outside, to a canyon or an alley, or try an empty room indoors. Make some sounds, and listen for an echo. Imagine it is God calling you. What might God be saying to you?

My class went on a hike the other day.
We climbed to the top of a mountain,
and I shouted H - E - L - L - O!
I heard a voice call back
   H - E - L - L - O!
It sounded just like my voice —
only far away.

My teacher said the sound I heard
was an echo.
It was fun to hear our own voices —
We kept calling out, and the sound
from space kept calling back.

I wonder what God's voice sounds like.
   Is it deep and gruff?
   Is it soft and gentle?
   Is it loud or quiet?
I think God keeps calling out and maybe
we are the sound that calls back.
   Maybe people are God's echo.

How are you God's echo?

What does God call us to do?

Sometimes an echo doesn't have to be a sound. When we copy what another person is doing, we are "echoing" their actions.

Play an echo or mirror game with a friend: Stand facing each other. One person starts to make a movement, and the other imitates it, just as if they were a reflection in a mirror.

We read in **1 Samuel 3** about God calling a young boy named Samuel to be God's helper. God calls us to be helpers, too.

What happens when you call someone, and they don't hear you, or they don't answer? How do you feel?

How do you think God feels, when we don't listen to God, or when we don't respond?

If you have a kite, you might fly it and feel the power of the wind.

Make a pinwheel: Mark the center of a 6" square of paper. Cut a line from each corner to about 1/4" from the center. Bend the corners to the center, and poke a straight pin through them; poke the pin through a small button, and then stick it into the eraser of a pencil. Blow on the pinwheel or move it in the air, and watch the wind make it spin.

When the wind blows warm, making grass, trees and flowers dance, it makes my hair brush against my face.

I think the wind is God's breath moving through the world, making it come alive.

What does God's voice sound like?
Psalm 29 talks about God having a voice as loud as thunder. Can you make a sound like thunder? I Kings 19:12 tells of God's voice being small and quiet. What is the tiniest whisper you can make? When and where do you hear God's voice?

I think I hear God's voice when _____

Have you ever heard an echo? Go outside, to a canyon or an alley, or try an empty room indoors. Make some sounds, and listen for an echo. Imagine it is God calling you. What might God be saying to you?

My class went on a hike the other day.
We climbed to the top of a mountain,
and I shouted H - E - L - L - O!
I heard a voice call back
   H - E - L - L - O!
It sounded just like my voice —
only far away.

My teacher said the sound I heard
was an echo.
It was fun to hear our own voices —
We kept calling out, and the sound
from space kept calling back.

I wonder what God's voice sounds like.
   Is it deep and gruff?
   Is it soft and gentle?
   Is it loud or quiet?
I think God keeps calling out and maybe
we are the sound that calls back.
   Maybe people are God's echo.

How are you God's echo?

What does God call us to do?

Sometimes an echo doesn't have to be a sound. When we copy what another person is doing, we are "echoing" their actions.

Play an echo or mirror game with a friend: Stand facing each other. One person starts to make a movement, and the other imitates it, just as if they were a reflection in a mirror.

1

We read in **1 Samuel 3** about God calling a young boy named Samuel to be God's helper. God calls us to be helpers, too.

What happens when you call someone, and they don't hear you, or they don't answer? How do you feel?

How do you think God feels, when we don't listen to God, or when we don't respond?

If you have a kite, you might fly it and feel the power of the wind.

Make a pinwheel: Mark the center of a 6" square of paper. Cut a line from each corner to about 1/4" from the center. Bend the corners to the center, and poke a straight pin through them; poke the pin through a small button, and then stick it into the eraser of a pencil. Blow on the pinwheel or move it in the air, and watch the wind make it spin.

When the wind blows warm, making grass, trees and flowers dance, it makes my hair brush against my face.

I think the wind is God's breath moving through the world, making it come alive.

What does God's voice sound like?
Psalm 29 talks about God having a voice as loud as thunder. Can you make a sound like thunder? I Kings 19:12 tells of God's voice being small and quiet. What is the tiniest whisper you can make? When and where do you hear God's voice?

think I hear God's voice when _____

Have you ever heard an echo? Go outside, to a canyon or an alley, or try an empty room indoors. Make some sounds, and listen for an echo. Imagine it is God calling you. What might God be saying to you?

My class went on a hike the other day.
We climbed to the top of a mountain,
and I shouted H - E - L - L - O!
I heard a voice call back
     H - E - L - L - O!
It sounded just like my voice —
only far away.

My teacher said the sound I heard
was an echo.
It was fun to hear our own voices —
We kept calling out, and the sound
from space kept calling back.

I wonder what God's voice sounds like.
     Is it deep and gruff?
     Is it soft and gentle?
     Is it loud or quiet?
I think God keeps calling out and maybe
we are the sound that calls back.
     Maybe people are God's echo.

How are you God's echo?

What does God call us to do?

Sometimes an echo doesn't have to be a sound. When we copy what another person is doing, we are "echoing" their actions.

Play an echo or mirror game with a friend: Stand facing each other. One person starts to make a movement, and the other imitates it, just as if they were a reflection in a mirror.

We read in **1 Samuel 3** about God calling a young boy named Samuel to be God's helper. God calls us to be helpers, too.

What happens when you call someone, and they don't hear you, or they don't answer? How do you feel?

How do you think God feels, when we don't listen to God, or when we don't respond?

Make a pinwheel: Mark the center of a 6" square of paper. Cut a line from each corner to about 1/4" from the center. Bend the corners to the center, and poke a straight pin through them; poke the pin through a small button, and then stick it into the eraser of a pencil. Blow on the pinwheel or move it in the air, and watch the wind make it spin.

If you have a kite, you might fly it and feel the power of the wind.

When the wind blows warm, making grass, trees and flowers dance, it makes my hair brush against my face.

I think the wind is God's breath moving through the world, making it come alive.

Hearing and Speaking 3

What does God's voice sound like?
Psalm 29 talks about God having a voice as loud as thunder. Can you make a sound like thunder? I Kings 19:12 tells of God's voice being small and quiet. What is the tiniest whisper you can make? When and where do you hear God's voice?

I think I hear God's voice when _____

Have you ever heard an echo? Go outside, to a canyon or an alley, or try an empty room indoors. Make some sounds, and listen for an echo. Imagine it is God calling you. What might God be saying to you?

My class went on a hike the other day.
We climbed to the top of a mountain,
and I shouted H - E - L - L - O!
I heard a voice call back
    H - E - L - L - O!
It sounded just like my voice —
only far away.

My teacher said the sound I heard
was an echo.
It was fun to hear our own voices —
We kept calling out, and the sound
from space kept calling back.

I wonder what God's voice sounds like.
    Is it deep and gruff?
    Is it soft and gentle?
    Is it loud or quiet?
I think God keeps calling out and maybe
we are the sound that calls back.
    Maybe people are God's echo.

How are you God's echo?

What does God call us to do?

Sometimes an echo doesn't have to be a sound. When we copy what another person is doing, we are "echoing" their actions.

Play an echo or mirror game with a friend: Stand facing each other. One person starts to make a movement, and the other imitates it, just as if they were a reflection in a mirror.

We read in **1 Samuel 3** about God calling a young boy named Samuel to be God's helper. God calls us to be helpers, too.

What happens when you call someone, and they don't hear you, or they don't answer?
How do you feel?

How do you think God feels, when we don't listen to God, or when we don't respond?

If you have a kite, you might fly it and feel the power of the wind.

Make a pinwheel: Mark the center of a 6" square of paper. Cut a line from each corner to about 1/4" from the center. Bend the corners to the center, and poke a straight pin through them; poke the pin through a small button, and then stick it into the eraser of a pencil. Blow on the pinwheel or move it in the air, and watch the wind make it spin.

When the wind blows warm, making grass, trees and flowers dance, it makes my hair brush against my face.

I think the wind is God's breath moving through the world, making it come alive.

What does God's voice sound like?
Psalm 29 talks about God having a voice as loud as thunder. Can you make a sound like thunder? I Kings 19:12 tells of God's voice being small and quiet. What is the tiniest whisper you can make? When and where do you hear God's voice?

think I hear God's voice when _____

Have you ever heard an echo? Go outside, to a canyon or an alley, or try an empty room indoors. Make some sounds, and listen for an echo. Imagine it is God calling you. What might God be saying to you?

My class went on a hike the other day.
We climbed to the top of a mountain,
and I shouted H - E - L - L - O!
I heard a voice call back
    H - E - L - L - O!
It sounded just like my voice —
only far away.

My teacher said the sound I heard
was an echo.
It was fun to hear our own voices —
We kept calling out, and the sound
from space kept calling back.

I wonder what God's voice sounds like.
    Is it deep and gruff?
    Is it soft and gentle?
    Is it loud or quiet?
I think God keeps calling out and maybe
we are the sound that calls back.
    Maybe people are God's echo.

How are you God's echo?

What does God call us to do?

Sometimes an echo doesn't have to be a sound. When we copy what another person is doing, we are "echoing" their actions.

Play an echo or mirror game with a friend: Stand facing each other. One person starts to make a movement, and the other imitates it, just as if they were a reflection in a mirror.

We read in 1 **Samuel** 3 about God calling a young boy named Samuel to be God's helper.
God calls us to be helpers, too.
What happens when you call someone, and they don't hear you, or they don't answer?
   How do you feel?
 How do you think God feels, when we don't listen to God, or when we don't respond?

 If you have a kite, you might fly it and feel the power of the wind.

 **Make a pinwheel: Mark the center of a 6″ square of paper. Cut a line from each corner to about 1/4″ from the center. Bend the corners to the center, and poke a straight pin through them; poke the pin through a small button, and then stick it into the eraser of a pencil. Blow on the pinwheel or move it in the air, and watch the wind make it spin.**

When the wind blows warm, making grass, trees and flowers dance, it makes my hair brush against my face.

I think the wind is God's breath moving through the world, making it come alive.

What does God's voice sound like?
Psalm 29 talks about God having a voice as loud as thunder. Can you make a sound like thunder? I Kings 19:12 tells of God's voice being small and quiet. What is the tiniest whisper you can make? When and where do you hear God's voice?

think I hear God's voice when _____

Have you ever heard an echo? Go outside, to a canyon or an alley, or try an empty room indoors. Make some sounds, and listen for an echo. Imagine it is God calling you. What might God be saying to you?

My class went on a hike the other day.
We climbed to the top of a mountain,
and I shouted H - E - L - L - O!
I heard a voice call back
    H - E - L - L - O!
It sounded just like my voice —
only far away.

My teacher said the sound I heard
was an echo.
It was fun to hear our own voices —
We kept calling out, and the sound
from space kept calling back.

I wonder what God's voice sounds like.
    Is it deep and gruff?
    Is it soft and gentle?
    Is it loud or quiet?
I think God keeps calling out and maybe
we are the sound that calls back.
    Maybe people are God's echo.

How are you God's echo?

What does God call us to do?

Sometimes an echo doesn't have to be a sound. When we copy what another person is doing, we are "echoing" their actions.

Play an echo or mirror game with a friend: Stand facing each other. One person starts to make a movement, and the other imitates it, just as if they were a reflection in a mirror.

We read in **1 Samuel 3** about God calling a young boy named Samuel to be God's helper. God calls us to be helpers, too.

What happens when you call someone, and they don't hear you, or they don't answer?
How do you feel?

How do you think God feels, when we don't listen to God, or when we don't respond?

Make a pinwheel: Mark the center of a 6" square of paper. Cut a line from each corner to about 1/4" from the center. Bend the corners to the center, and poke a straight pin through them; poke the pin through a small button, and then stick it into the eraser of a pencil. Blow on the pinwheel or move it in the air, and watch the wind make it spin.

If you have a kite, you might fly it and feel the power of the wind.

When the wind blows warm, making grass, trees and flowers dance, it makes my hair brush against my face.

I think the wind is God's breath moving through the world, making it come alive.

Make music! If you have a wind instrument (a recorder, trumpet, flute, kazoo, etc.) play it and imagine that it is God's breath moving through you that makes the sound. Or, make some rhythm instruments: put pebbles, sand, rice, or beans between two paper plates and staple them together. Make drums from old coffee cans with plastic lids. Pound a nail through some bottle caps, and nail them to an old piece of wood. Use your imagination to make other instruments; decorate them with markers, paint, streamers, etc.

I think that God's breath moves through me, too.

That makes me special,
   having a little bit of God inside me.

That makes everyone special,
   having God's breath inside them.

We can make words and music with God's breath.

What kind of words and music does God's breath make?

Walking home this afternoon,
I heard the wind whistle,
   a dog bark,
   a bird chirp,
   a baby cry.

All these sounds —
   some soft
   some loud.
They are God's song.

If you sang a song to God, what would you sing?

Sing this song. Once you get used to the rhythm and the pattern, make up some more verses. You might want to play some rhythm instruments, or move your body to the beat of the music.

(Sung to the tune of "Michael, Row Your Boat Ashore")
God we thank you for your love, hallelujah.
God we thank you for your love, hallelujah.

We are called to do God's work, hallelujah...

God made rocks and trees and streams, hallelujah...

Help us, God, to do good deeds, hallelujah...

When we're sad, you dry our tears, God we thank you...

God is with us all the time, hallelujah...

When we're happy or we're sad, God is with us.
When we're cheerful or we're mad, God is with us.

4   Copyright © 1999 by Jewish Lights Publishing. All rights reserved. No part of this kit may be reproduced or transmitted in any form or by any means, electronic or mechanical, including photocopying, recording, or by any information storage and retrieval system, without permission in writing from the publisher. Printed in Mexico.

Make music! If you have a wind instrument (a recorder, trumpet, flute, kazoo, etc.) play it and imagine that it is God's breath moving through you that makes the sound. Or, make some rhythm instruments: put pebbles, sand, rice, or beans between two paper plates and staple them together. Make drums from old coffee cans with plastic lids. Pound a nail through some bottle caps, and nail them to an old piece of wood. Use your imagination to make other instruments; decorate them with markers, paint, streamers, etc.

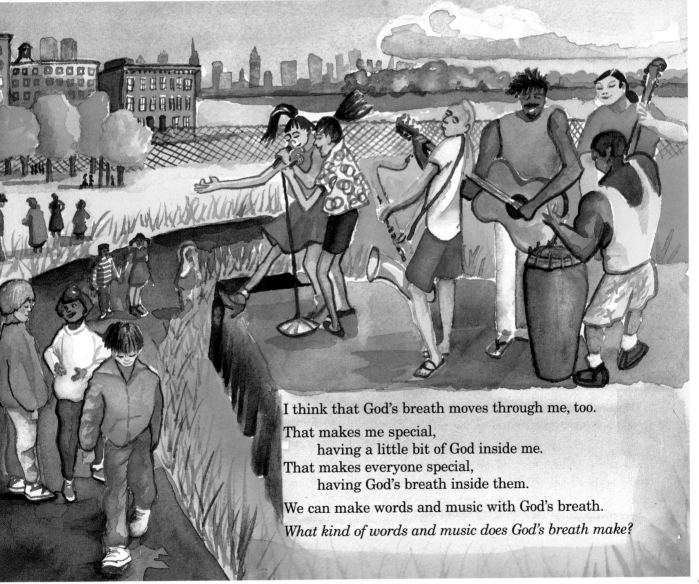

I think that God's breath moves through me, too.

That makes me special,
     having a little bit of God inside me.
That makes everyone special,
     having God's breath inside them.

We can make words and music with God's breath.

What kind of words and music does God's breath make?

Walking home this afternoon,
I heard the wind whistle,
    a dog bark,
    a bird chirp,
    a baby cry.

All these sounds —
    some soft
    some loud.
They are God's song.

If you sang a song to God, what would you sing?

Sing this song. Once you get used to the rhythm and the pattern, make up some more verses. You might want to play some rhythm instruments, or move your body to the beat of the music.

(Sung to the tune of "Michael, Row Your Boat Ashore")
God we thank you for your love, hallelujah.
God we thank you for your love, hallelujah.

We are called to do God's work, hallelujah...

God made rocks and trees and streams, hallelujah...

Help us, God, to do good deeds, hallelujah...

When we're sad, you dry our tears, God we thank you...

God is with us all the time, hallelujah...

When we're happy or we're sad, God is with us.
When we're cheerful or we're mad, God is with us.

4   Copyright © 1999 by Jewish Lights Publishing. All rights reserved. No part of this kit may be reproduced or transmitted in any form or by any means, electronic or mechanical, including photocopying, recording, or by any information storage and retrieval system, without permission in writing from the publisher. Printed in Mexico.

Make music! If you have a wind instrument (a recorder, trumpet, flute, kazoo, etc.) play it and imagine that it is God's breath moving through you that makes the sound. Or, make some rhythm instruments: put pebbles, sand, rice, or beans between two paper plates and staple them together. Make drums from old coffee cans with plastic lids. Pound a nail through some bottle caps, and nail them to an old piece of wood. Use your imagination to make other instruments; decorate them with markers, paint, streamers, etc.

I think that God's breath moves through me, too.

That makes me special,
    having a little bit of God inside me.
That makes everyone special,
    having God's breath inside them.
We can make words and music with God's breath.

What kind of words and music does God's breath make?

Walking home this afternoon,
I heard the wind whistle,
   a dog bark,
   a bird chirp,
   a baby cry.

All these sounds —
   some soft
   some loud.
They are God's song.

If you sang a song to God, what would you sing?

Sing this song. Once you get used to the rhythm and the pattern, make up some more verses. You might want to play some rhythm instruments, or move your body to the beat of the music.

(Sung to the tune of "Michael, Row Your Boat Ashore")

God we thank you for your love, hallelujah.
God we thank you for your love, hallelujah.

We are called to do God's work, hallelujah...

God made rocks and trees and streams, hallelujah...

Help us, God, to do good deeds, hallelujah...

When we're sad, you dry our tears, God we thank you...

God is with us all the time, hallelujah...

When we're happy or we're sad, God is with us.
When we're cheerful or we're mad, God is with us.

4 Copyright © 1999 by Jewish Lights Publishing. All rights reserved. No part of this kit may be reproduced or transmitted in any form or by any means, electronic or mechanical, including photocopying, recording, or by any information storage and retrieval system, without permission in writing from the publisher. Printed in Mexico.

Make music! If you have a wind instrument (a recorder, trumpet, flute, kazoo, etc.) play it and imagine that it is God's breath moving through you that makes the sound. Or, make some rhythm instruments: put pebbles, sand, rice, or beans between two paper plates and staple them together. Make drums from old coffee cans with plastic lids. Pound a nail through some bottle caps, and nail them to an old piece of wood. Use your imagination to make other instruments; decorate them with markers, paint, streamers, etc.

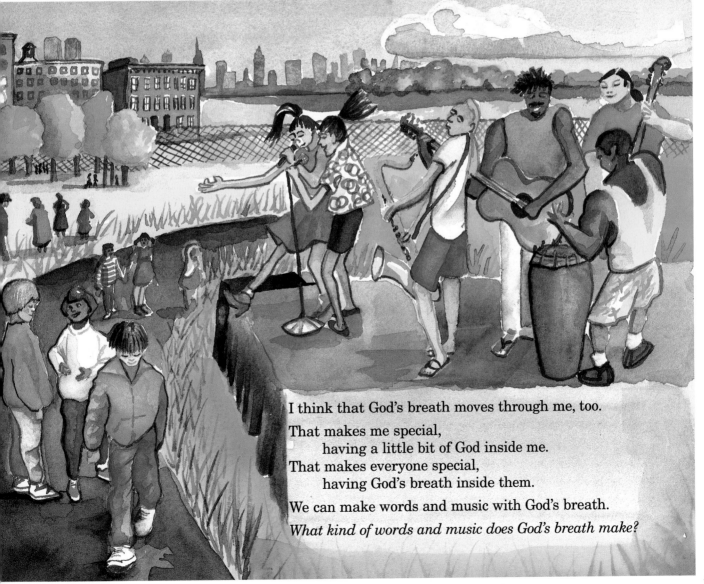

I think that God's breath moves through me, too.

That makes me special,
    having a little bit of God inside me.
That makes everyone special,
    having God's breath inside them.

We can make words and music with God's breath.

What kind of words and music does God's breath make?

Walking home this afternoon,
I heard the wind whistle,
a dog bark,
a bird chirp,
a baby cry.

All these sounds —
some soft
some loud.
They are God's song.

If you sang a song to God, what would you sing?

Sing this song. Once you get used to the rhythm and the pattern, make up some more verses. You might want to play some rhythm instruments, or move your body to the beat of the music.

(Sung to the tune of "Michael, Row Your Boat Ashore")

God we thank you for your love, hallelujah.
God we thank you for your love, hallelujah.

We are called to do God's work, hallelujah...

God made rocks and trees and streams, hallelujah...

Help us, God, to do good deeds, hallelujah...

When we're sad, you dry our tears, God we thank you...

God is with us all the time, hallelujah...

When we're happy or we're sad, God is with us.
When we're cheerful or we're mad, God is with us.

4   Copyright © 1999 by Jewish Lights Publishing. All rights reserved. No part of this kit may be reproduced or transmitted in any form or by any means, electronic or mechanical, including photocopying, recording, or by any information storage and retrieval system, without permission in writing from the publisher. Printed in Mexico.

Make music! If you have a wind instrument (a recorder, trumpet, flute, kazoo, etc.) play it and imagine that it is God's breath moving through you that makes the sound. Or, make some rhythm instruments: put pebbles, sand, rice, or beans between two paper plates and staple them together. Make drums from old coffee cans with plastic lids. Pound a nail through some bottle caps, and nail them to an old piece of wood. Use your imagination to make other instruments; decorate them with markers, paint, streamers, etc.

I think that God's breath moves through me, too.

That makes me special,
  having a little bit of God inside me.
That makes everyone special,
  having God's breath inside them.

We can make words and music with God's breath.

What kind of words and music does God's breath make?

Walking home this afternoon,
I heard the wind whistle,
   a dog bark,
   a bird chirp,
   a baby cry.

All these sounds —
   some soft
   some loud.
They are God's song.

If you sang a song to God, what would you sing?

Sing this song. Once you get used to the rhythm and the pattern, make up some more verses. You might want to play some rhythm instruments, or move your body to the beat of the music.

(Sung to the tune of "Michael, Row Your Boat Ashore")
God we thank you for your love, hallelujah.
God we thank you for your love, hallelujah.

We are called to do God's work, hallelujah...

God made rocks and trees and streams, hallelujah...

Help us, God, to do good deeds, hallelujah...

When we're sad, you dry our tears, God we thank you...

God is with us all the time, hallelujah...

When we're happy or we're sad, God is with us.
When we're cheerful or we're mad, God is with us.

4   Copyright © 1999 by Jewish Lights Publishing. All rights reserved. No part of this kit may be reproduced or transmitted in any form or by any means, electronic or mechanical, including photocopying, recording, or by any information storage and retrieval system, without permission in writing from the publisher. Printed in Mexico.

Make music! If you have a wind instrument (a recorder, trumpet, flute, kazoo, etc.) play it and imagine that it is God's breath moving through you that makes the sound. Or, make some rhythm instruments: put pebbles, sand, rice, or beans between two paper plates and staple them together. Make drums from old coffee cans with plastic lids. Pound a nail through some bottle caps, and nail them to an old piece of wood. Use your imagination to make other instruments; decorate them with markers, paint, streamers, etc.

I think that God's breath moves through me, too.

That makes me special,
    having a little bit of God inside me.
That makes everyone special,
    having God's breath inside them.

We can make words and music with God's breath.

What kind of words and music does God's breath make?

3

Walking home this afternoon,
I heard the wind whistle,
　　a dog bark,
　　a bird chirp,
　　a baby cry.

All these sounds —
　　some soft
　　some loud.
They are God's song.

If you sang a song to God, what would you sing?

Sing this song. Once you get used to the rhythm and the pattern, make up some more verses. You might want to play some rhythm instruments, or move your body to the beat of the music.

(Sung to the tune of "Michael, Row Your Boat Ashore")

God we thank you for your love, hallelujah.
God we thank you for your love, hallelujah.

We are called to do God's work, hallelujah...

God made rocks and trees and streams, hallelujah...

Help us, God, to do good deeds, hallelujah...

When we're sad, you dry our tears, God we thank you...

God is with us all the time, hallelujah...

When we're happy or we're sad, God is with us.
When we're cheerful or we're mad, God is with us.

4　Copyright © 1999 by Jewish Lights Publishing. All rights reserved. No part of this kit may be reproduced or transmitted in any form or by any means, electronic or mechanical, including photocopying, recording, or by any information storage and retrieval system, without permission in writing from the publisher. Printed in Mexico.

Make music! If you have a wind instrument (a recorder, trumpet, flute, kazoo, etc.) play it and imagine that it is God's breath moving through you that makes the sound. Or, make some rhythm instruments: put pebbles, sand, rice, or beans between two paper plates and staple them together. Make drums from old coffee cans with plastic lids. Pound a nail through some bottle caps, and nail them to an old piece of wood. Use your imagination to make other instruments; decorate them with markers, paint, streamers, etc.

I think that God's breath moves through me, too.

That makes me special,
        having a little bit of God inside me.
That makes everyone special,
        having God's breath inside them.

We can make words and music with God's breath.

What kind of words and music does God's breath make?

Walking home this afternoon,
I heard the wind whistle,
    a dog bark,
    a bird chirp,
    a baby cry.

All these sounds —
    some soft
    some loud.
They are God's song.

If you sang a song to God, what would you sing?

Sing this song. Once you get used to the rhythm and the pattern, make up some more verses. You might want to play some rhythm instruments, or move your body to the beat of the music.

(Sung to the tune of "Michael, Row Your Boat Ashore")

God we thank you for your love, hallelujah.
God we thank you for your love, hallelujah.

We are called to do God's work, hallelujah...

God made rocks and trees and streams, hallelujah...

Help us, God, to do good deeds, hallelujah...

When we're sad, you dry our tears, God we thank you...

God is with us all the time, hallelujah...

When we're happy or we're sad, God is with us.
When we're cheerful or we're mad, God is with us.

4   Copyright © 1999 by Jewish Lights Publishing. All rights reserved. No part of this kit may be reproduced or transmitted in any form or by any means, electronic or mechanical, including photocopying, recording, or by any information storage and retrieval system, without permission in writing from the publisher. Printed in Mexico.

Make music! If you have a wind instrument (a recorder, trumpet, flute, kazoo, etc.) play it and imagine that it is God's breath moving through you that makes the sound. Or, make some rhythm instruments: put pebbles, sand, rice, or beans between two paper plates and staple them together. Make drums from old coffee cans with plastic lids. Pound a nail through some bottle caps, and nail them to an old piece of wood. Use your imagination to make other instruments; decorate them with markers, paint, streamers, etc.

I think that God's breath moves through me, too.

That makes me special,
    having a little bit of God inside me.
That makes everyone special,
    having God's breath inside them.

We can make words and music with God's breath.

What kind of words and music does God's breath make?

3

Walking home this afternoon,
I heard the wind whistle,
    a dog bark,
    a bird chirp,
    a baby cry.

All these sounds —
    some soft
    some loud.
They are God's song.

If you sang a song to God, what would you sing?

Sing this song. Once you get used to the rhythm and the pattern, make up some more verses. You might want to play some rhythm instruments, or move your body to the beat of the music.

(Sung to the tune of "Michael, Row Your Boat Ashore")

God we thank you for your love, hallelujah.
God we thank you for your love, hallelujah.

We are called to do God's work, hallelujah...

God made rocks and trees and streams, hallelujah...

Help us, God, to do good deeds, hallelujah...

When we're sad, you dry our tears, God we thank you...

God is with us all the time, hallelujah...

When we're happy or we're sad, God is with us.
When we're cheerful or we're mad, God is with us.

4   Copyright © 1999 by Jewish Lights Publishing. All rights reserved. No part of this kit may be reproduced or transmitted in any form or by any means, electronic or mechanical, including photocopying, recording, or by any information storage and retrieval system, without permission in writing from the publisher. Printed in Mexico.